Writing Well
in School
and Beyond

Michael Berger

Cover art © 2013 by S. R. Berger

ISBN: 978-1491053751

Printed in Charleston, South Carolina, USA
CreateSpace Independent Publishing Platform
www.createspace.com/4334252

For instructor exam/desk copies, email request to
michaelberger.wwsb@gmail.com

To Andrea

Contents

Fundamentals

What Good Is Writing?

Here are some benefits of writing well, aside from getting good grades on papers you have to write in school:

- You can put your voice out in the world and people will hear and respond to you. This applies not only in school and college, but also in your
  o personal life.
  o work life.
  o public life as a citizen.
- Writing is a studying and learning tool. It is good not only for sharing what you know but also for learning it in the first place. It helps you process information more effectively and organize your knowledge.
- Writing reinforces your knowledge. Writing a paper about a subject helps you to know it better.

In short, writing is a way to project your voice and to gather, organize, consolidate and integrate learning.

Writing is also an essential and marketable life skill. In the world outside of school, talking and writing are the number one reflection of knowledge and the quality of your thought. Are there multiple choice tests in real life? No, in real life when you are asked to apply or demonstrate your knowledge, you will either do something or say it or write it. Learning to write it well helps you also to be able to say it more powerfully and persuasively.

The goal of your high school teachers is to prepare you for college or for employment, while the goal of your college teachers is to prepare you for professional employment or further study in graduate school. But they also have other goals. They also aim to prepare you for

- advancement and leadership in your profession.
- lifelong learning and participation in communities that value and use written communication regularly.

The English Composition course in college, or the senior English Language Arts class, is designed to prepare you for the world of "higher learning." This means that the thinking and writing you're expected to do should go beyond the surface of things, beyond the rote level, beyond gathering and comprehending information to analysis, evaluation, synthesis, application of knowledge. Your teachers are interested in developing your "critical thinking" abilities. This means being more precise, deep, careful and flexible with your ideas and language. It means figuring out the assumptions underlying your and others' arguments, making logical inferences based on limited information, using and testing evidence, and checking your own and others' motives, attitudes and biases.

In all these crucial goals and activities, writing plays a central role. Learning to write well is essential to your achieving these goals and participating in the learning process effectively and productively.

What Is Good Writing?

Many people have a limited notion of what good writing is. We tend to think it means literary, flowery, fancy, sophisticated, pretty language. This kind of writing, we often think, is for people who are or who want to be "writers," and so it doesn't matter to me. It's the stuff of *Literature* with a capital L, and not the concern of those of us who don't aspire to be writers of fiction and poetry. But this limited notion fails to recognize how writing is important and useful for all. As citizens, students, and workers in all sorts of career fields that have nothing to do with fiction and poetry or journalism, we are members of groups or communities for whom writing is an important activity and skill. In these communities, we are expected to be clear, informative, polished and persuasive; not only do others expect this of us, but we get greater satisfaction by being so. We need to be able to produce effective language for practical situations we find ourselves in as citizens, in our personal lives, and certainly as students all across the curriculum, not just in English classes. Writing well advances individual thinking and enables the sharing of knowledge. We need to be able to compose informational and argumentative writing effectively, no matter our chosen field. We must be able to put together claims, reasons and evidence in logical and persuasive ways. Writing well in this sense, not to make novels and poems, but to make clear, meaningful, persuasive explanations and arguments, is everyone's business. We all need to produce "good writing" and be "good writers."

Myths about Writing

There are some ideas about writing that seem true but are not. Believing these myths hampers our ability to develop as writers. Here are a few of the worst ones:
1. *Good writing comes easily to good writers.*
2. *Excellent writers are born with a gift or talent that others don't have. Writing well is a genetic gift.*
3. *My ability as a writer is limited. There's a ceiling on what I can do.*

We tend to think that the published writing we admire, which seems so expert and polished, and the best writing among our peers as students and workers, is so good because writing comes easily to those who produce it. They don't have to struggle like we do with writing; it just flows from them; they are gifted with this ability through their genetic endowment. They can accomplish great things with language—they're just good at it, while I am not. But this is not true. The good writing we see is usually the product of lots of effort; it doesn't come easily at all. Rather, just the opposite: the writer has worked and reworked and reworked the piece of writing many times to make it look so good. "Good writers" practice and develop their skill, while we assume our skill level is pretty much set and therefore don't work at developing it. But the fact is, when you think of "good writing" not as fancy fiction or poetry but as clear, direct, logical explanations and arguments, you can develop your ability to produce this kind of writing way beyond your current level of skill. Writing well is not a genetic endowment, and there is no ceiling on what you can do as writer. This doesn't mean that it will someday become magically easy for you, as you imagine it is for "good writers." No—the "good writers" work even harder at it than we do. But you can get better and better and better as a writer, with practice.

What Kind of Skill Is Writing?

Writing in school or college is often thought of as similar to taking a multiple-choice test, as an alternative way of assessing student knowledge. You might have to take an exam or you might have to write a paper: two ways for the teacher to see what you know. But writing a paper is really a very different activity from a multiple-choice exam. Rather than thinking of writing as an alternative kind of exam to test your concept comprehension, it's more accurate and helpful to think of it as a performance. It's analogous to a clinical performance in the health sciences, where a nursing student or a medical student has to apply his or her knowledge and skill in some clinical activity to assess or heal a patient. Likewise, writing is a performance that can be evaluated according to standards of proficiency that measure your command of knowledge and ability to apply that knowledge in a situation requiring judgment and skill and thinking on your feet.

Or writing is like a sport, where you bring together various sub-skills to achieve a recognizable level of performance in a game situation, applying a body of knowledge with judgment, making decisions to achieve goals. In a sport like tennis, for instance, you start to learn the forehand or backhand swing in stages, through sub-skills, gradually. First you very consciously place your feet and twist your body in certain ways, practicing the basic postures over and over until you can do them accurately and they get into your muscle memory. Your tennis coach will tell you exactly how to hold the racket and twist your wrist when you swing. In the beginning you have to be conscious of every element and tell yourself to do it just so. As you practice under coaching, your sub-skills develop and come together, so that eventually you can make a good swing, performing all the elements accurately but no longer having to think about them separately at the conscious level. So with writing: you will need to go through the steps of the writing process consciously and purposefully at first, gradually developing the sub-skills to the point where you can instinctively move through them and put them together effectively in response to different writing situations.

Other analogies also are helpful to understand the nature of writing as a learnable skill. Learning to write is like learning to play music. Can you imagine a capable musician who has listened to very little music? No, listening to lots of music is a prerequisite for playing it well. When you listen to music, you get it in your system and you develop a feel for it, for how it works when you like it, what makes it good. You develop a feel for rhythm, melody, harmony, tone, patterns, for how it all comes together to make your feet bounce and heart dance. Good musicians are first of all good listeners who learn a lot through hearing how the music they like works. Likewise, good writing—and we're talking here about the kind of writing we all must do well, not writing great novels but writing clear memos and emails and papers—builds upon a foundation of reading. When you read a lot, you learn how language works effectively. You develop a feel for the rhythm, word choice, phrasing, tone, sentence structures, and essay patterns that work effectively for you as a reader . . . and so, as a writer you learn how to reproduce some of those effective techniques and strategies in your own writing. The funny thing is, as you learn to do that you get to enjoy your own writing just like you enjoy good writing by others. It doesn't come easy, but when it works, there's a great satisfaction. And that further motivates you to develop your writing skill.

Many people think that learning to write in school and the workplace is like learning to ride a bicycle, as if it's something you get the hang of once, and from then on you go at it pretty much automatically. But learning to write is not like learning to ride a bicycle in that sense. Rather, it's like learning to ice skate. What happens when you learn that activity is a gradual process of moving from awkward and slow to graceful and quick. When you start learning to ice skate, your movement is very awkward and difficult. At first you can't get started. Then once you get started, you can't keep your balance and fall down a lot. Then you are able to stay up, but you can move only slowly, without adjusting speed or direction. After a while, with steady practice, you can glide fairly smoothly and rhythmically and you can stay up without falling, but you can't do much else. Then, with continued effort, you start to learn how to change direction and speed while keeping your balance, and as you get better you can develop some real style and begin to move more gracefully. As your skills develop, you can do some fancy footwork, shifting one foot over the other while moving sideways, turning to skate backward, even jumping, eventually moving just about any way you can imagine within the rules of flexibility for the human body. . . . Well, learning to write is like that, too. It's not a matter of learning one template or method, like riding a bike, but more like developing the ability to move from awkward and slow composing, uncertain of what is expected and how to deliver it, to being able to size up a writing situation and develop a smoothly finished product that delivers what's needed. It's a gradual process, in which you become more sure on your feet and more graceful and powerful, by degrees, as you develop.

Expectations in College and Work Life

The expectations of academic and workplace readers of your writing, and of fellow citizens in public and political life, are not those of a recreational reader. They want clear and organized writing that fulfills a specific purpose in a specific writing situation. Communicating effectively in college and at work calls for greater precision, complexity, and idea development than what was expected in your previous school settings. In order to achieve such qualities in your writing, you have to really appreciate the difference between writing and talking. Writing well in this sense is more than just putting on the page what you have to say about a subject. Talking allows for flexible exploration, but the level of precision and depth of thought is less in talking than can be achieved in writing. Talking is *emerging* thought, while writing, if you approach it effectively, is *crystallized* thought. The act of writing enables you to develop and refine your ideas into a form that is sharper, clearer, fuller and better organized than the ideas that come out when you're just talking out your ideas on a subject. This is true, however, only if you approach writing effectively. If you approach writing as just transcribing on the page what you would say into the air, then you won't reap the advantages writing offers. The key to transforming your emerging good, but rough, ideas in speech into a great, clear and powerful written expression, a more refined version of those ideas, is . . . **revision**.

Revision is the essential part of the writing process for collegiate and workplace writing (and often for effective personal and public communication as well). Just as there are basic myths about writing that hamper the developing writer, there are also limited notions about revision that hold people back from achieving their potential as writers.

What Is Revision?

First off, you must understand what revision, truly speaking, is not. Revision is not editing—it's not finding a better word here and there, fixing grammar and punctuation mistakes. As one of my colleagues says, revision is more like moving the furniture than dusting it. Revision and editing are two very different activities, even though they are often confused as being one and the same.

This misunderstanding about the nature of revision is basic to one approach to writing—which we might call the *linear* model of writing. In this approach, you go through a series of steps in your writing process where after each step is completed you go on to the next one, and you never go back and revisit previous steps. The linear model of writing typically looks something like this: analyze assignment → prewrite → plan (probably including an outline with very symmetrical features like three main points and three supporting points under each main point) → draft according to outline → "revise" to finish up and polish the piece of writing. Now, I've put quotation marks around that *revise* to indicate that under this model of writing, that stage is called "revision" but in practice what goes on in that stage doesn't really deserve the name *revision*. Just fixing a few things is not really revising; it's editing. So, under this linear model of writing, there really isn't any revision to speak of at all. When we write according to this approach, we get none of the advantages of true revision.

Another model of the writing process is one we might call *recursive*. To recur means to happen over again. A recursive approach is one in which you can go back and reconsider features of your writing that reach deeper than changing a word here and there or fixing a grammatical problem. The word *revision* itself suggests what you can do using this approach: re-vision, re-seeing. You can gain a different view of your discussion or argument or story. You can go back and reconsider what your main point is, how to say it better, which parts of your discussion are strong and which need development, what you might add to fill out your discussion in a better way, either because in your initial draft you didn't quite capture something important or because you shifted your focus or main idea and new elements are needed to flesh out that idea. You can revamp your plan to reflect your new focus, prewrite and draft new material, and revisit your phrasing in many parts of your discussion to express your ideas more clearly or to get rid of some of the deadwood and fuzzy phrasing that may have come out the first time you tried to express your idea.

Here's a model of a recursive writing process, with arrows flowing in both directions across several phases:

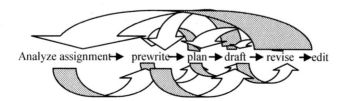

Analyze assignment➔ prewrite➔ plan ➔ draft ➔ revise ➔edit

Using a recursive writing process allows us to refocus, reshape and rephrase our writing, as much as we like, until it really comes out clear and powerful.

The idea of going back over your writing may make you feel that you're not a good writer. But we all have the experience of trying to put down on the page what we're thinking and not quite getting it down to our satisfaction (or in a way that our reader can readily understand). Beginning writers think only they have this problem with their initial drafts. This is a myth about writing. It isn't that expert writers can just sit down and type out a polished draft on the first try because they're "good writers." Their first drafts are also rough and full of false starts and detours and tangles and unclear parts. But what experienced writers are able to do that beginning writers don't do is revise extensively. It seems counterintuitive, but actually strong writers revise *more* than beginning writers. *That's* what makes their writing strong!

A professor of composition did a study that provides a lot of helpful insight into just what kind of revision goes into effective writing. In the study, Nancy Sommers took a group of experienced writers and a group of college freshmen writers and compared their revision strategies as they took three papers through three draft stages each. In addition to tracking the kinds and frequencies of changes each writer made in their drafts, Sommers and her research team interviewed the participants to see how they described their approaches to revision. You can see by the bar graphs below how the two groups of writers compared. Notice that the experienced writers made many more changes in their drafts than did the student writers. Again, this seems counterintuitive, but the results of this study accurately reflect the basic truth about writing: better writers revise more. Also notice the *kinds* of changes that each group made. The student writers mostly changed their texts at the word level, not at sentence or paragraph or theme level. And the student writers mostly cut

Kinds of Operations
Experienced Writers: 1994 Operations
Beginning Student Writers: 333 Operations

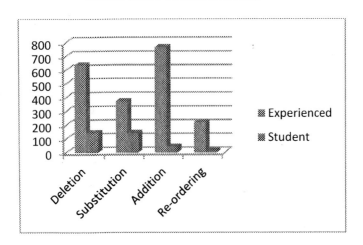

Level of Operations
Experienced Writers: 1994 Operations
Beginning Student Writers: 333 Operations

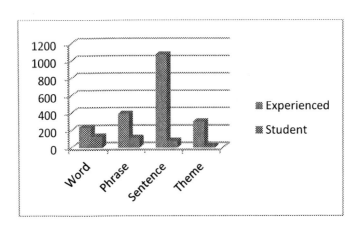

and replaced words; they rarely added new material or reordered existing material. In contrast, experienced writers do a lot of adding and reordering of material, and they make lots of changes at the sentence and theme level. This kind of revision is what goes into making their writing more effective than the writing of people who just change their drafts by cutting or swapping some words here and there and fixing grammar and punctuation.

It's also interesting to see how the two groups of writers talk about what they're doing when they examine and revise their drafts. Experienced writers say things like this about revision:

- "It is a matter of looking at the kernel of what I have written, the content . . . responding to it, making decisions, and actually restructuring it."

- "In one draft, I might cross out three pages, write two, cross out a fourth, rewrite it, and call it a draft. I am constantly writing and rewriting."

- "Rewriting means on one level, finding the argument, and on another level, language changes to make the argument more effective. . . . There is always one part of a piece that I could keep working on. It is always difficult to know at what point to abandon a piece of writing. I like this idea that a piece of writing is never finished, just abandoned."

- "My first draft is usually very scattered. In rewriting, I find the line of argument. After the argument is resolved, I am much more interested in word choice and phrasing."

- "It means taking apart what I have written and putting it back together again. I ask major theoretical questions of my ideas, respond to those questions, and think of proportion and structure . . . I find out which ideas can be developed and which can be dropped. I am constantly chiseling and changing as I revise."

In contrast, student writers say things like this:

- "I read what I have written and cross out a word and put another word in; a more decent word or a better word."

- "Reviewing means just using better words and eliminating words that are not needed."

- "I don't use the word rewriting because I only write one draft and the changes that I make are made on top of the draft. The changes that I make are usually just marking out words and putting different ones in."

You might say that experienced writers are able to see the forest as well as the trees, while beginning writers, once they've set down the main lines of their discussion, don't think about the big picture anymore and just get to work on words here and there, and doing very limited kinds of things with them. When they're asked what they're doing in revising, the student writers talk about *correcting* and *fixing* their writing. These activities are more properly called *editing*. So in this sense, as I suggested above, these writers are actually not *revising* in a meaningful way at all. When the experienced writers are asked what they're doing in revising, they talk about big-picture, conceptual things: *finding the line of the argument, restructuring the shape of the discussion, finding the implied seed buried under the surface of the draft.* Their approach goes to show that effective writers feel the need to revise significantly and that they do so. If you feel that you need to revise your paper significantly, congratulations! That insight is the first step toward becoming a highly effective writer. It's not a sign that you're a "bad" writer because it's a need felt by all writers. What separates the successful writer from the novice is, strangely enough, not the need to revise in the first place, but the willingness to go through with revising in a big way. Good writers work harder at their writing, not easier. And they've got their eye on the big picture. Or, rather, the way it works is that they mainly have their eye on the big picture for most of the writing process, and then after they've shaped and reshaped and reshaped their writing in big, conceptual ways, they turn their eye toward the details for clarifying, smoothing, polishing and correcting. It's this last bit of fixing up, which comes after considerable revision has already taken place, which is what beginning writers limit themselves to and call "revision," but it's really only editing.

If you're not revising like that, in a sense you're not really writing; you're just transcribing speech on the page. Remember the distinction I made above, between *emerging thought* and *crystallized thought*? Putting down one draft and then fixing it up a bit with some editing is simply transcribing your emerging thought. Whatever you put down need not be your last word on the subject, but rather just your first. In order to shape it and polish it so that it crystallizes to a clear, precise, powerful and persuasive piece of writing, you have to revise your initial draft, maybe several times, if you want to write as effectively as experienced and successful writers do, because that is exactly what they do. It's not that once they become experienced and good at writing, they don't need to change their drafts anymore—they continue to do so, sometimes even more than they did in the past, as through experience they gain strategies and insight about how to make writing more effective.

This kind of writing, the product of deep revision, is what we're looking for in college level writing and the workplace. It is this *recursive* approach to writing, revising your material in big-picture ways through multiple drafts, that enables that celebrated activity called *critical thinking*. Effective revision enables you to make the expression of your ideas precise, deep, careful, flexible. It enables you to identify and articulate assumptions, make inferences, elaborate evidence, and analyze ideas and arguments effectively.

It is simply not possible to achieve this level of writing and thinking by following a template like the five-paragraph theme, where you have to have three main points and each point is supported by two minor supporting points, and so on, with an introduction that presents a thesis statement with your three main points and a conclusion to round off the essay. When this pre-fabricated form for essays is used in combination with the linear approach to writing, the writer gets boxed in and confined by the template. In this approach, the thinking that writing enables is actually prevented. You can't think your way through an idea by revising if you determine in advance that you will have three main points and don't think any further about them. What if your idea really has two main points, or four? When form determines content, you can't develop or refine your ideas. You're stuck with your emerging thought in its initial form. Content should determine form. Then you can follow your ideas where they lead and develop them further. This is scary for someone who has always had that form to rely on, but the ability to think through an idea in a natural way and develop a form to the writing that really expresses that idea is exciting and liberating. Using only the five-paragraph theme leads you to think of writing as an artificial activity in which you have to rely on fluff and bull to fill out the form. It saps the excitement of genuine thinking out of the process, and that is a great loss for you as a student and as a person. Writing can be so much more than coming up with fluff and filling in a template. It can be as exciting and interesting as those conversations you have had with friends or family about the wonderful mysteries of life and things that really matter to you, where your mind is whirring with substance and possibilities and reaching for clarity and power. In order to make writing this exciting and powerful, you have to be able to revise, and in order to revise properly, you have to be free of templates like the five-paragraph theme that confine the natural order of ideas and make you invent artificial elements that have no place in your real thinking.

While the standard five-paragraph template for an essay of opinion or analysis is too rigid and confining, it may happen that sometimes your idea *does* naturally fit into five paragraphs. There's nothing wrong with that. And it's also true that in various disciplines and work settings there are established structures for papers, reports, or memos; for instance, the science lab report has a definite set of sections that you are required to present in order, and other academic and professional disciplines have similar structures their practitioners are expected to follow. But even within those guidelines, you will still want to revise and sometimes discover radically different ways to focus and develop your discussion.

Writing and Thinking

Taking the theme of thinking further, let's do some more myth-busting: what is the relation between thinking and writing? Our initial notion is that writing is the expression of thinking. We think, and then we write down our thoughts. But writing is not simply an expression of thinking. Writing is a way to develop and enhance thinking . . . but only if it's done using an effective recursive process. *Linear* writing, as described above, sets your thinking in a box from the get go. *Recursive* writing does not confine thinking in that way; it liberates and promotes thinking. Your thinking will improve as you learn a process for discovering, arranging, focusing, clarifying and crystallizing your thought more effectively. It's not an exaggeration in this sense to say that, not only does writing enable thinking, writing *is* thinking. When you write this way, what you're doing when you revise your material *is* thinking. To write more effectively is to develop a system for improved thinking, making your ideas more clear, developed, deep and complex. Not just their expression on the page, but their shape and substance in your mind as well.

Assumptions of Effective
Teaching and Learning of Writing

Your English Language Arts and College Composition teachers strive to enable you to write with confidence and without apology. No one who graduates from high school or participates in higher learning in college should have to say, "I hope you like my paper OK and it gets a passing grade. I'm just not a good writer. It's not my thing." You should be able to get down on the page a precise and powerful version of what you're trying to say, writing that is clear, effective and compelling. Remember, if it doesn't come out that way the first time, that's par for the course. Revise it, and revise it some more and more, until it becomes what you're striving to think and say. Writing, in our civilization, is everybody's thing—not creative writing necessarily, but clear, effective explanations and analyses and arguments, which are the currency of our professional, social, political and commercial life together, just as paper money (or the debit and credit card balances that represent our monetary wealth) is what circulates as the basis of our economy. Everyone participates in the circulation of language, much of it written. To participate in that circulation with mastery and effect, contributing your voice as you see fit, is a primary goal of education.

Your teachers and classes can help you develop as a writer by assuming that

- everyone can improve,
- we can reduce the frustration and increase the satisfaction in writing,
- development in critical reading goes hand-in-hand with learning to write well, and
- we all need practice and individualized coaching to develop as writers.

If you're lucky, your English classrooms will include many opportunities for interactive, workshop activities and lots of feedback and practice writing.

For guidance, you have to rely on your teachers and courses and academic opportunities in the form of paper assignments in English and other courses. But there are also some things you can do on your own that will help you become a stronger writer. There are two essential activities that can help you grow in power and grace as an "ice skater," to use the analogy mentioned above:

1. Write. . . . Practice writing regularly, all kinds:
   - formal
   - informal
   - personal
   - academic
   - professional
   - especially expository and argumentative (making and supporting claims)

2. Read . . . a lot. Again, read all kinds of writing, including whatever floats your boat for entertainment. But also, to work on your craft as a writer, read especially non-fiction prose that makes arguments and analyzes complex ideas. This way you'll get the logic, structure, strategies and rhythms of such writing in your subconscious mind and so develop your own repertoire of successful approaches and techniques, just as musicians develop their chops by listening to a lot of music. Ask your teachers (not only English, but also history, social studies, philosophy, etc.) and other trusted adults for recommendations, and join them in conversation about what you read. (Conversation also plays a crucial role in writing, to set up the questions you address and to clarify your ideas in both

brainstorming and revising phases of your writing process.)

Advice

1

Learning to write well is a developmental process—there are no simple templates nor a simple body of facts to master once and then you're done. Also, learning to write well involves not only things to digest and practice, but also perspectives and attitudes that will help you become more effective and successful.

2

What is writing? Writing is a process of generating structures of language and then making decisions to shape ideas for processing by a reader, in order to fulfill the writer's specific purpose . . . it's a complex process of decision making. On one hand there is a flow of ideas, and on the other hand there is wrestling your own language for clarity and fitness to thought, a process that enables depths of thinking not otherwise available. Writing clearly proves that you've thought clearly, as eating pudding is proof of its taste. Successful writing provides the joy of accomplishment when your thought is clarified.

3

This kind of writing is possible only through revision. In revision, you should have a big, glorious mess. Revision creates a productive dynamic between emerging thought and crystallized thought, as discussed above. Our motto should be: draft fearlessly, revise vigorously. The Nobel Prize-winning scientist Linus Pauling said there are two parts of genius: generate an abundance of creative ideas, and discriminate among them to find the ones worth developing.

Most people in high school and college have never written up to their ability because they have not fully used the writing process, and they lack an enabling attitude toward revision. Many students perform writing assignments like plopping clay on a wheel and forming it a bit and handing it in. In order to make a decent pot or vase out of clay, you have to do a lot more than just plop down the clay and call it a pot. You have to do an initial rough shaping, then spin the wheel and work and rework the shape and substance, maybe even sometimes taking away big chunks of clay, and maybe along the way also allowing the process to feed your imagination with a different and improved vision of what you're trying to create. That's an image of how the writing process works and how writing is thinking.

4
FINDING THE LINE OF YOUR ARGUMENT

Sometimes you're able to do this at the start of drafting through an outline and thesis statement. But sometimes you need a full draft, with details and development of one line of thought, to check and test, in order to find your best line of argument. A typical process for doing this might follow these stages:

- Explore the issue for yourself through a draft.
- Discover a more effective line of argument somewhat hidden in the draft which may be different from your initial intention.
- Develop and refine this improved line of argument.
- Revise accordingly, shaping the argument for the reader as well as for yourself, adding and cutting a lot of material and reordering and rephrasing many sentences.

This requires tremendous discipline to see objectively what is actually in your draft and not interpret it as what you intended. What we intend rarely gets on the page clearly in one draft.

We need to be able to see what's really there so we can change and develop it accordingly. That's why it's so valuable to have conversations about your writing with others. They provide an objective eye on your draft and draw out your thinking in more productive ways.

5
WRITING CENTER

If your school or college has a writing center or writing lab, use it! Go there for feedback on your drafts, help with brainstorming, and clarification of assignments. The writing center is an extremely valuable resource for student writers. If your school does not yet have a writing center, persuade your teachers and administrators to establish one!

6
READING

Read to see how writers do it. Some specific things to read for:

- transitions
- topic sentences
- paragraph development
- setting up an idea (background/context/relevancy)
- finishing off an idea (conclusion)

Also: We read not only to hear others' ideas but also to stimulate our own. Responding to thoughtful and well-expressed writing of others improves our writing, as our tennis or basketball game is lifted by playing with a talented opponent.

7

Read quite a bit in physical print form. You can mark up the texts with your own thoughts more easily, and it's harder to develop sustained concentration and textual smarts reading online. It can be done, but it's harder due to distractions. It's like reading a book when bound up with the book in the same volume are letters from friends, marketing flyers, magazine articles, bits of entertaining comic strips, still photos from movies and TV shows, favorite comedy routines, and other odd miscellanea. The distractions disable the sustained focus and concentration needed for deep thought.

8

Make writing fun for you. Practice on subjects you enjoy. Write school papers extremely well, so you experience the joy of craft. The fact is, everyone can excel at writing, as long as we're talking about writing explanatory and argumentative essays, the kind of writing we have to do in school and at work. We can shift the bell curve, so that the average quality of writing is much better than what it is now. What excellence feels like at first is messy hard work. If more and more rising American citizens learn how to go through that messy hard work, our work life and public life will improve. You can contribute in the future by making writing fun for you and practicing a lot now.

9

Propose the following deal to your teacher: If you get a letter to the editor or a guest op-ed column published in your local newspaper, you get a free pass on a course assignment (if there is a final exam, maybe even on that!). You should bargain for super-duper extra credit for getting a letter or column published in a national newspaper like the *New York Times* or *Wall Street Journal* or *Washington Post* or *USA Today*.

10

The order in which things occur to you in drafting is not necessarily the best order for your reader to process your ideas most clearly and effectively. You are free to re-order your material. This is one of many reasons revision is so helpful for writing effectively.

11

Your teacher might give you various kinds of assignments that are useful for developing different skills and areas of writing competence:

- short assignments to work on grammar, punctuation and mechanics (*local issues*).
- short assignments to work on style.
- complete papers (with revision).

Try to treat each kind of assignment with equal attention and care, even the short ones.

12

Your teacher might show you models of the assignment you're being asked to write . . . ideally samples that show high performance, medium and low. And ideally, more than just one sample of a high paper. That way you can know that there are more ways than one to do the assignment successfully—you can see the samples as models that show good features of successful papers that are achievable in various ways rather than as blueprints to be done in exactly the same mold. It's possible to hold different opinions, for example, and write equally well, or to present an objection and rebuttal to an argument in various places in the structure of the paper. If your teacher does show you models of sample student papers, take advantage of the opportunity to get clearer on what you're being asked to do by studying the samples closely and trying to revise your own paper to reflect the same kinds of desired features and strengths in your own way. Ask questions to determine what variations on the model are acceptable and what particular features make a sample high or medium or low.

13
SOURCE DOCUMENTATION

Your textbook and online resources will instruct you in detail on content and format requirements in documenting your sources. Here are a few really urgent requirements for you to master as you're getting a handle on all the format wrinkles:

- When you use a source citation format such as APA or MLA, which requires in-text citations, these are the essential elements you need to include in your text:
    - the name of the author (or title of work if there is no human or corporate author given).
        - The element you must use in your text is the one that appears at the left margin of the alphabetical list of references at the end of your paper (this list is called *References* in APA and *Works Cited* in MLA).
    - page(s) where the reader can find the material cited, if the source is a print source (in APA, this is needed only for quotations, not summaries or paraphrases).
    - the date of publication (in APA).
- If you quote material, use a *signal phrase* to introduce the material. Failure to use this signal phrase results in a *dropped quotation*. You should look up both of these terms in your writer's handbook or online resources for source documentation.
- When you summarize, and sometimes when you paraphrase, you are free to place the author's name in the parentheses. This way of citing summaries allows your voice more prominence even while you

present sourced material, instead of always saying "According to so-and-so . . . "

- When you're integrating sources, don't start or end a paragraph with quotes. Frame the discussion in your own voice. (See the next item.)

14

Many of your academic writing assignments (and workplace writing assignments, too, in many fields of work) require you to do research and cite sources in your paper. There are lots of formatting details to get straight when you do that, but another important consideration is maintaining your own voice while incorporating source material. One helpful concept to keep in mind is the idea of the "frame." You will provide an introduction and conclusion to your discussion that frames the discussion: you set up the topic in the beginning and then you drive home your main idea at the end. Your voice should dominate these frame structures. Particularly when you incorporate a lot of source material into your discussion, you also want to be sure your voice is heard at the beginnings and endings of paragraphs.

Within the body of the discussion, you have further opportunities to adjust your reader's focus and expectations with transitional comments and setting up the context and meaning of the source material. It's important to keep your eye (and ear) on maintaining your voice as the guiding voice the reader hears, setting up the discussion, reinforcing its importance, and steering the reader's understanding and responses throughout.

In addition to establishing an appropriate frame for your source-based discussion and guiding the reader with transitions, another way to maintain your voice is to rely less on quotations to incorporate source material and more on paraphrase. Paraphrasing is hard to do well, and there are risks in doing it weakly and then running into the problem of unintended plagiarism. So, it's a sub-skill of academic and workplace writing you should focus on; seek out guidance on it from your teachers and textbooks and online resources.

15
ARGUMENT

Teachers and scholars mean something very particular by the term *argument*, which is much broader than what we mean in everyday language when we use that word. Our everyday sense is that an argument involves hostility and the desire to vanquish an opponent, presenting reasons to support our view and maybe calling names and shouting. *Argument* in an academic or workplace setting has the same sense of requiring logical support for your view, but it's gentler and less egotistical, and oriented more toward discovering what's true and supportable than toward winning. When we make an argument in this sense, we're not hostile. And while the point is to persuade, it is not to win at all costs. Rather, the aim is to get at the truth of the matter as we see it, admitting that when the issue is complex and many-sided, there may be modifications of our view that take other points of view into consideration. In academic and workplace discussion, such modifications are called *qualifications* or *qualifiers*. To *qualify* your claim means to modify it, usually by making it more narrow and specific to certain cases, or admitting that other considerations require you to modify your claim by including elements of other views. In argument in this sense, we don't express anger or hostility toward others, and we hold ourselves to the same standards of fair reasoning in support of our claims as we hold others to when they're supporting claims with which we disagree. Practicing this kind of argument prepares us for democratic citizenship, and doing so enables us to improve our own ideas and arguments, making them clearer, deeper, and even more persuasive.

16

You communicate with many different groups of people joined by shared interests or activities. These various groups you belong to may be associated with a particular field of work or subject of interest or cultural identity, and they each have particular ways of organizing and presenting their ideas. Each such community addresses other members of the community in its own way. Regardless of your academic or vocational interests, you already participate in a number of such groups, including your family, your friends and classmates, and your age cohort (each generation has its own slang and other language conventions). The academic world has its own ways of using language and expectations associated with the expression of ideas, and within that general set there are communities of particular disciplines or areas of study. As you go on in your academic career, you will be schooled by the professors and advanced students in the communication expectations and practices of your field. Different professions and sectors of society also have their own communication practices. Doctors speak and write in a certain way, as do lawyers and advertisers and marketers and show-business people and athletes and carpenters and plumbers and construction workers and journalists and political consultants and ethnic groups and churches. Part of learning a trade or profession is learning its terminology and its expectations and practices in communication (note the similarity between *communication* and *community*—that suggests how they are related). We speak and write somewhat differently for each community we're involved in—for instance, you wouldn't talk with your grandparents about a concert or sports event you saw in the same way that you would with your friends. Learning to write with purpose and audience awareness enables you to move smoothly among various communities and make your writing and speech appropriate and effective in each situation. You then will be able to adopt an appropriate voice for each group you communicate in, in terms of

- level of formality (sometimes called *register*).
    - For instance, I've adjusted my register in writing this guidebook to make it somewhat more conversational than most academic and scholarly writing. In most academic and many professional writing situations, you'd want to avoid using contractions, although in some of those situations, contractions and informal words like *okay* might be okay. Part of being an effective writer is judging the level of formality most appropriate for your purpose in the given situation.
- conventions of format and mechanics.
- ways of using and presenting evidence.
- ways of using and presenting data.

17

Learning to write appropriately in college is like learning to get around in a new culture. In academic culture in American colleges and universities, you will face various patterns of papers and varying emphasis on what's important in the writing, and in different disciplines you'll be required to write in different modes, such as narrative, descriptive, comparison/contrast, or analyzing a process in history or science or a technical field, or making an argument. You have to be able to shift into effective modes of communication in these various communities and writing situations.

Argument is a dominant mode that appears widely across disciplines. Learning to argue in the academic and professional sense is also needed in a democracy. One of the things you learn to do in college and the workplace is approach topics not out of the blue but against the background of an ongoing conversation about those subjects. Very often in these situations, we read and hear what others have said and then respond to that with our analyses and opinions. One recent textbook identifies the most basic "move" in academic writing as "They Say/I Say." We first indicate what the topic of conversation is and particular things that have been said on the topic, and then we present our contribution or assessment. Getting comfortable with this basic move goes a long way toward making you an effective communicator and thinker in academic and workplace writing communities.

18

Your teacher may instruct you in *logic*. A basic assumption of our civilization is that our arguments should be logical. Some training in the basic principles of logic is useful. This is not to make you an expert in logic the way a philosophy major must be, but in the same way that clearly supporting claims in writing is everybody's business, not just English majors, so learning a bit about the basic principles of logic is essential in order to make our arguments clear, accurate and persuasive. Teachers of composition typically train their students in one or both of two ways of analyzing logic. You may run across these approaches to logical argument in textbooks or lectures:

1. The *syllogism*
2. The *Toulmin System*

The system of the syllogism, dating back to the ancient Greeks, is more formal and difficult, but very useful. The Toulmin System takes the way people usually argue in everyday life, and even in college and the workplace, and shows how the logic of those strategies works. When you get to logic in your studies, work at it thoroughly and get a good grounding in it. Your own thinking will be clearer and more powerful. You'll find it very beneficial for your academic and work life, and also it will help you persuade others to agree with you in your personal life! And you will be less likely to be a victim of the tricks and smokescreens of politicians and others bent on taking advantage of you.

19
THE BEST TWO THINGS YOU CAN DO TO IMPROVE YOUR WRITING

If you meet this challenge, I bet you will raise your grade on writing assignments by at least a full grade point:

- read at least one well-written, well-edited magazine article or newspaper column per day.
- write one page in a journal per day.

Do this for 8-12 months and you're guaranteed to raise your grade, and what's more, gain more confidence and satisfaction in your writing and reading.

20
PARAGRAPHS

A note on organizing paragraphs: Paragraphs are idea packages. They should be neat and clean in terms of the number of topics they contain. How many topics should each paragraph contain? One. Often our writing drifts, or our mind is moving faster than our writing, and so when we're drafting, topics blend together within one paragraph. It's important when reviewing your draft to be ready to revise whenever you spot more than one topic per paragraph. It's devilishly hard to spot sometimes, since we review our writing through our initial intentions and cannot see so easily how the reader will process what we put on the page, so this is something you need to remember and be keen about when reviewing your drafts. Discussing your draft with an experienced reader can help you spot the drifting likely to be present in your draft paragraphs.

21

Another thing about paragraphs: Paragraphs make claims. Just as an argument or analysis essay has an overall major claim or central idea, each paragraph makes a mini-claim as part of an argument that supports the main claim. Your job in the paragraph is to persuade the audience the claim is justified. Think of the audience as the best readers and thinkers among your peers, a group who is also skeptical of your claim. Don't just lay out the claim and leave it at that: go to some length to persuade them with details, examples, further explanations, and so on. Always including exactly three supporting points in the paragraph, each with its own minor support, is not the best way to do this. Content should drive structure, not the other way around.

22

Ideas should progress from the beginning to the end of a paragraph—don't say things repetitively. Arrange the elements of paragraphs in an effective and logical order for the reader to get your point most clearly; revise if the order of ideas seems out of whack. In revision, also insert links between one idea and the next with precise transition words and phrases. Give your reader a hand to let them know the way ideas are related.

23

On summarizing: there are two ways to summarize. The most common is to boil down into a concise statement what the writer is saying. But another way is especially useful when you're summarizing a piece of writing that has a persuasive or analytical purpose: use *doing* language. An everyday version of this is when you report on conversation between family members or friends. Don't we often say things like this: "She was trying to get him to go with her. But he didn't buy her story and he questioned her motive, asking her why she had gone to Joey's house if she felt that way . . ." See how this way of summarizing a conversation uses doing language? *Trying to get him to go . . . he didn't buy . . . he questioned her motive, asking her . . .* All this is doing language. It gets at the purpose of the conversation and the intended effects on listeners, while indicating the content in relation to the purpose. When we do this same kind of thing in summarizing things we read for school or work, we can more easily and deeply get at the purpose and meaning of what we're talking about. It makes us think about the writer's purpose and how his or her writing works, which gives us a firmer grip on the content and meaning and allows us to talk about it in ways that relate more effectively to our own purpose in writing.

24
FICTION AND NON-FICTION

Don't confuse the terms *story* and *essay*. A story is a short work of fiction and an essay a short work of non-fiction. A story is a narrative with characters and plot. An essay is usually not a chronological telling of incidents involving a character or characters. An essay explains or explores ideas or experiences, but not in terms of character and plot development. A non-fiction account of events and incidents might look like a story, but if it is a relation of things that actually happened it will probably be called an essay. The book-length equivalents of these two categories are *novels* and *non-fiction books*. Books of history do tell stories, but they're accounts of what is thought to have actually happened, not made-up stories, so they're referred to as non-fiction books rather than novels. Also, a novel is by definition fiction, so it's redundant to say *fictional novel*.

25
READ ACTIVELY

Just as conversation is essential to effective academic and workplace writing (see 4 above), so also is reading an important part of writing well. If we have to write about something we read, we should approach the reading itself in a more effective way than just letting our eyes go over the words on the page and thinking about their significance as we go. This passive approach gives us a much less powerful grip on what we're reading than we can get, just as following a linear approach in writing is less powerful than a recursive method. Instead, we should read actively. This means marking the text, writing in the margins, recording your own thoughts and responses and making notes that organize and improve your grasp on the material. Your composition textbook should have some advice and examples about how to do this. Also see this essay by Mortimer Adler on active reading: http://chuma.cas.usf.edu/~pinsky/mark_a_book.htm

When we read actively, we set ourselves up for a highly effective review and deeper grasp of the reading, we engage in a conversation with the author that spurs our thinking, and we get some good notes going that can flow into the actual writing we have to do.

26
TURN YOUR TOPIC INTO A QUESTION

When your assignment requires you to have a thesis statement, here's a way to approach the topic that can help you generate a sharp thesis: turn your topic into a question. Then, when you set about writing your response to the topic, you can have a question to answer, and the answer to the question becomes your thesis.

27

STATE YOUR THESIS DIRECTLY

When you write a thesis statement, do not simply indicate what the topic of the discussion is, but state at the outset precisely what your position is. That is, not "In this paper I will tell you my position on x and support it." Don't just signal that you're going to tell me your position. Instead, actually tell me your position: "My position on x is this: _____." Then the purpose of the paper is to support that position. And, since you will use a recursive writing process to deepen, reshape and refine your argument, the thesis statement will need to be revised *after* you've revised the body of the paper. Teachers and bosses love to see a coherent argument with a precise thesis statement that matches exactly what the body of the paper turns out to be.

28

Test your thesis statement: it should sound like the answer to a question. Answer the question directly, with the same expectation for focus and directness you hold yourself to in speaking when someone asks you a direct question. Let's say someone asks you this question: "What do you think about policy X, which your state legislator is proposing?" Would your answer in conversation be this sort of thing: "I'm going to tell you my opinion about policy X"? No, you'd come right out and say it: "I agree/disagree with policy X because . . . " Just so, your thesis statement should not simply announce the intention to address the topic the question is about—the thesis statement should actually be a direct answer to the question. But realize that it won't come out that way at first; nevertheless, ultimately the final product should have a clear, direct, precise thesis statement. Again: revision is needed and beneficial.

29

Your topic and thesis may evolve as you go through a recursive writing process and think through your ideas with increasing precision and power. You should allow this benefit of the writing process to affect your ideas and how you phrase them. You may frame your topic along certain lines initially, based on your original motive and how you begin thinking about your topic. But through further thinking and research (and conversation), you can refine your topic; you shift or sharpen the focus, and then the initial framework is no longer relevant; it becomes a limiting and misleading way to approach, define and express your topic. When this happens, we often allow ourselves to be stuck with the baggage of the initial framework. We need to be flexible and sharp to redefine our focus.

- It helps to turn the topic into a new question and discipline ourselves to answer that new question in a fresh way instead of carrying on with the old answer to the initial question.
- Then we need to allow that fresh approach free play throughout a new draft. This could mean a total overhaul and elimination of much previous material, reordering material that stays, adding whole new sections and new bits here and there, and rephrasing in some places. All this helps to sharpen the draft along a new line, with a new focus.

30

DRAFTING TO DISCOVER

You draft and revise the body of the paper in order to nail down the thesis. You start with a tentative thesis to give your writing focus and direction, but you remain open to the deeper, more refined, more complex, or even different direction your draft moves in. Then you go back and reformulate the thesis to capture the increased refinement and complexity your revision has revealed.

31

Your composition textbook may include case studies in revision. Or your teacher might provide examples of how students have revised their writing through two or more draft stages. Study these carefully and take them to heart as models of how you can approach your writing to radically improve the results beyond your first draft. Look especially carefully at how the focus shifts or the main idea changes or gets refined as the writer moves through the revising process. When you revise this way, you will find yourself doing some of the following:

- Recognize elements of your first draft other than your thesis that offer a better, deeper, clearer way to envision your topic and express the thesis. In other words, ideas that first come out at the margins of the writing turn out to be more significant than what you initially conceived as your central idea.
- This means then that you need to *add* new material along those sharper lines and rearrange material you already have, so that you refocus your writing into a new shape.
- It also means that you can change the relations of ideas and the emphasis different parts receive. A mark of advanced skill, which you will eventually learn to do, is to be able to adjust emphasis among elements in a discussion.
- It also means you are probably cutting things out, and you should do this ruthlessly.
- As you go through this process, discuss, discuss, discuss your draft and your ideas beyond the draft, and allow the free discussion to inform revision of your draft.

32

A writing process tip: leave easy fruit for the start of the next session. When you've made some progress in your work, leave something to start on next time that is pretty easy and satisfying to do. Then you'll get some momentum going that will make it easier for you to tackle the next major challenges.

33

Format work is detail work. Get the details down right. There are two main reasons to do source documentation and other format issues well:

- Your readers need you to document sources so they can check or follow up on your sources and have resources for their own work. It's a matter of consideration and professionalism.
- Your ability to do the detail work carefully and accurately reflects on you. If you can do it well on papers, this is evidence that you can attend to important details in your job well. In the same way, if you can't do the details well in documenting sources and so on, this is evidence that you may not be able to do detail work well in your career. People notice.

34

Experienced writers imagine a reader. This helps them make effective decisions about content, organization, strategies, voice and style. This means:

- Assignments your teachers give you should help you imagine a reader (if not in the form of a particular person, at least by the concerns and expectations your imagined reader has). If an assignment doesn't already do this, ask your teacher for guidance regarding your reader's concerns and expectations.

- You should think about the imagined reader and learn to diagnose problems and make decisions for that reader (not "what should I put here?" but "what does my reader need?").
- As you gain experience with people who give useful feedback on your drafts, you can begin to anticipate their typical responses and concerns. You will learn gradually to see your draft material through their eyes and so gain some objectivity on your own material. Then you can write for them as your reader. Working steadily with writing-center tutors is often very helpful in this way.

35

Rhetorical questions are not often effective in academic writing. They can be fun, and they work well as snappy comments in casual conversation, but in a formal argument they cut logic short by merely implying what you should make explicit and elaborated.

36
ELEMENTS OF STYLE: SYNTAX

Listen to the following series: I came, I had seen, I did conquer.

Compare that to this: I came, I saw, I conquered.

Which comes across stronger and clearer? The second version follows a pattern called *parallelism*. Its improvement over the first version demonstrates the power of sentence structure, also called syntax. Your teacher and textbook and other readings can provide abundant examples of excellent syntax. What's important to understand is that you always can decide to structure your sentences differently than the first way they come out on the page, and doing so can make a world of difference in the power and clarity and flow of your writing

37
ELEMENTS OF STYLE: DICTION

Just as you can decide to restructure sentences, you can also be more precise and powerful in selecting words. Excellent word choice, or diction, is more than having a varied and colorful vocabulary—it's more a matter of finding the precise word to mean exactly what you intend to say. As Mark Twain said, the difference between the right word and an approximate word is the difference between lightning and the lightning bug. Often a plain word is the best word—flowery language is not necessarily precise and powerful language. See Abraham Lincoln's famous short speeches for evidence of this, and many sentences of Hemingway, Twain, Churchill and Thoreau and many others. Consider this sentence from Thoreau: "I went to the woods because I wished to live deliberately, to front only the essential facts of life, and see if I could not learn what it had to teach, and not, when I came to die, discover that I had not lived." This is simple language but also very meaningful. Notice all the one-syllable words, which are not fancy but which together say precisely what the writer means. Learning the power of words and of precision in words comes from reading a lot and practicing writing.

38

Don't say *In my opinion, I believe . . .* or *In my opinion, I think . . .* When you do this, you're saying that you have only an opinion about what you believe, that you don't really know what you yourself think. This phrasing is redundant and confusing; it's verbally stepping over your own toes. Instead say *It is my opinion that . . .* or even better, *I think . . .* or *I believe . . .*

39

The purpose of an introduction is to set up your reader to be interested in your topic question, the answer to which is the thesis. How to do this effectively in any rhetorical situation depends on the audience and your specific purpose in writing. It pays to think about how to do it through considering audience and purpose rather than focusing on which clever gimmick, or "hook," to use. Another way to think about the introduction is to focus on establishing the context—defining the conversation that the essay contributes to, narrowing down to the question that the thesis is the answer to.

40

It often happens that your control of local issues (grammar and mechanics and so on) decreases when you move from informal narrative about yourself to argument. The language of argument is harder to control, and it's harder to get what you mean into the right words. Additionally, these issues of language become more difficult when you're also working to focus, develop and organize a logical argument. Because of the additional conceptual challenges of writing arguments or analyses, you will find your grasp of the surface level of your writing slipping. Be prepared for that, and once you work out the concepts and structure of your writing, go back and work extra hard and extra long on polishing up the surface again. The rewards of getting both levels working smoothly are immense, but you need to realize that it will take extra work and extra time.

41

When citing sources in formal writing, refer to authors the first time you mention them by last name, or first and last, never just by first name. After the first mention, you can use just the last name.

42

One of the most commonly violated punctuation rules: commas and periods go inside the end quotation mark. When the material being quoted is one or more full sentences, this makes sense. But when the quoted material is just a word or phrase, this is fussy and illogical, and the British do it the sensible way, placing the period or comma outside the quotation mark. But following this rule consistently is considered by proficient North American readers and writers to be a sign of know-how.

43

Struggling to form an argument need not be an exclusively solitary job. You can rehearse arguments, claims, evidence, issues, and objections through talk. It's quite magical the way existing ideas get clearer and new ideas pop out in conversation.

44

Your teacher might put you in small groups for peer feedback on your drafts. When you have this opportunity, remember the following:

- You want to support, not offend. It's like being a sparring partner or tennis practice-partner.
- Be always talking and sharing about your paper, even outside of class and with a variety of people. Keep the conversation going. You'll be amazed at what comes up in different conversations.
- Adjust your expectations for feedback, both giving and receiving: both ways, try to focus more on productive thinking-through rather than on being "right" or finished with your writing process.
- Realize that no first draft is ever ready to publish or present—critique is objectivity, not cruelty, helping the writer to gain a better sense of what's on the page

for the reader, to incorporate a reader's perspective. It's like helping a friend to understand a situation better when they're emotionally mixed up in it and you have some objectivity.

45

The effective writer's attitude is not "Can't I soon get done with this thing?" but rather with every draft and workshop here is another opportunity to develop and refine something into clearer form, better shape. If you adopt the first attitude instead of the latter, you will never write to your ability and you will get less satisfaction out of writing, even if you get to finish your papers more quickly.

46
WRITING BLOCKS

Do something else that requires little thinking, get working physically, get your energy moving and your mind distracted. But while you're doing that, be prepared to jump back onto your project when your subconscious mind delivers breakthrough ideas.

47

Dig up meanings of words you don't know and then wrestle with sentences in which they appear until they give up their sense to you. Grow intellectual muscle.

48

Reading in school and the workplace is not a recreational pastime. It requires a high degree of skill, dedication, effort, and sense of adventure. It pays to be a growing reader, always expanding your vocabulary and becoming increasingly capable of comprehending, interpreting and forming opinions in response to challenging writing. In order to grow as a writer, you must grow as a reader. You should be learning new words day by day, with a print dictionary that gets worn with use and a bookmarked dictionary web site that gets clicked on so much that your online advertisements become dominated with appeals to buy new dictionaries. You should become comfortable with increasingly complex and challenging reading, all the way up to the classics. Shakespeare's works contain 15,000 different words, while the King James Bible contains 5,000. If you can get a handle on Shakespeare and other classic writers, you can ride on top of the vocabulary of any writers you may meet in school or work rather than having their vocabulary riding on you.

49
Reading the classics of philosophy, history and literature is not a matter of taste; it's the duty of democratic citizenship. Our nation was founded on the assumption that voting citizens would be educated in the traditions, ideas and arguments at the root of our society. Not so you can agree with them or believe anything in particular or admire, but so you can know what the issues are and have the intellectual muscle to address them responsibly.

50
WORD SENSE
SENTENCE SENSE
Develop word sense and sentence sense . . . until you recognize when a sentence works well and when it doesn't. You should be able to notice many sentences in a first draft that don't work well and begin to understand the reasons why they don't, and develop a sense for possible solutions. This is not really a matter of correct grammar, but more a matter of clarity, precision, logic and flow.

51

"Writing well" is not the province of poets or fiction writers or journalists—it's for everyone. Not everyone needs to be an effective plumber, dancer, violinist, bicycle racer, electrician or nurse. But everyone needs to write well. We all use language in all aspects of our lives, and proficient use of language is a basic competency of work, citizenship and even personal development. You must have a "way with words"—this is not for poets only.

- Bad words kill relationships, good ones bring us close. Unclear words between healthcare practitioners kill patients; clear ones heal. The single most frequent cause of medical error is not technical mistakes but communication problems.
- Words we tell ourselves help or harm our sense of self and our understanding of our world.

52

Gaining clarity, focus and organization through revision *feels* like:

analogies to sport

- participating in a long series of volleys in tennis and making a final put-away shot
- moving down the sideline past defenders and toward the goal and placing a clever shot past the goalie in soccer or hockey
- passing the ball with speed and accuracy around the court and nailing a three-pointer in basketball
- running a play-action pass downfield for a touchdown in football
- figuring out and overcoming the defense in any team sport

analogies to daily life

- organizing a messy room

- finding the right arrangement for the layout of furniture in a room or house
- fixing a badly hung door
- unclogging a stuck pipe
- putting together a menu for a knockout meal
- resolving an interpersonal dispute
- finding your personal path forward after feeling stuck in some area of life
- deliberating on a problem and finding good reasons to make a tough decision with confidence

analogies to music and art
- playing the notes of a scale exactly right on a violin
- composing a killer verse or musical passage in a song
- coming to understand an effective compositional design for a painting or sculpture

analogies to math, engineering and science
- arriving at a solution to a difficult problem in algebra
- resolving a design dilemma in engineering
- realizing an effective design for a science experiment

. . . and all these are gained through creativity, hard work, practice and sincere application with skill and strategy. Writing well also takes hard work . . . and it may be a kind of work you've never done and need to learn how to do effectively. In the past, you may have handed in papers, but if they came out in only one draft, you didn't really "write" them. All these activities involve problem solving and decisions. So also with writing. Without putting your paper through multiple drafts, you're not giving yourself the opportunity to recognize problems and solve them; you're not allowing yourself to make decisions to improve on what first came out.

53

What is writing? Putting words down on a page, a way of expressing ideas? Yes, but it's more than that. It's a way of thinking. The words on the page are not the end result but the beginning of a process that leads to more clarity than originally intended, even to new ideas you didn't have before you put the words down.

54

Write when you're not writing—that is, even when you're not sitting at a desk with pad and pencil or keyboard, remember your writing project and be alert to the gifts of your subconscious as it works on the problems of writing under the conscious radar.

55

Start anywhere and get a lot of stuff down, then figure out what you really can say or need to say from what you've written down. Go from there, surpassing your initial writing as a springboard for the real stuff.

56

There is always a disconnect between what's in our head and what we put on the page. Having others respond helps us gain objectivity on what's there.

57

Writing is not just putting words on the page; it's also talking with others about what is on the page and what you intend. Feedback and revision: get feedback from others, and let the draft material talk back to you and help you understand your ideas better, so that you can then reshape (revise) what is on the page.

58

Your textbook or teacher may give you a list of procedures to follow when revising particular kinds of writing. Here is a caveat to that advice. *Caveat* is from Latin, meaning *warning*. It means an exception to a rule or a specific way in which a generalization doesn't apply. Here is the caveat:

All these tips from teachers and textbooks work, but simply referring to this list is ultimately not the best way to revise. Beginning plumbers, carpenters, engineers and other craftspeople refer to tips from experts for solving problems in their fields as they arise in their day-to-day work. But once they have developed a feel for the work, they refer to their own sense of what's needed more than to a generic list of operations. And so will you in your writing, once you've become empowered as a writer through experience and practice.

You can become an expert in academic writing, which in turn will enable you to be competent and effective in workplace writing (and personal writing, for that matter, too). Not everyone can be or wants to be a practicing poet or novelist, but all educated people should be *experts* in academic and vocational writing—and they all *can* be. . . *you can* be an expert.

59

WRITING IN A JOURNAL

See what words can do for you. Write on any subject, personal as well as academic and professional. Writing freely, you may find that the words on the page can guide and surprise you as much as you determine and control them. Articulating on the page concentrates your intention and perspective in a way that just ruminating in your mind does not. Your dialogue with yourself becomes more dynamic and then more precise.

60

Pose questions to yourself that bother or confuse you, and write yourself into clarity. You'll learn a lot this way about how writing relates to thinking and about how to express yourself clearly.

61

BEN FRANKLIN'S TECHNIQUE

The great American statesman, diplomat, and scientist Ben Franklin was also a great writer. He helped Jefferson with the Declaration of Independence, and his autobiography is considered a classic of American literature. Young Ben used a technique to develop his writing ability that you could use, too, if it appeals to you.

Ben would take a prose passage from an essay he admired and turn it into poetry. After setting his version aside for a few weeks, he would look at it again and turn the poetry back into prose, working on his style as he went. Then he could compare his new prose version to the original essay: in many cases he noticed phrasing and technique by the original author that he could learn from in order to improve his own style. In some cases, he thought his version was an improvement over the original! In both cases, he was learning to improve his own style. If you try this yourself, you will see ways to improve your style, and it can be fun to play with language this way. No grades, no evaluation—just flexing your own writing muscles and dancing with language for a while.

See old Ben Franklin's explanation of this exercise strategy here:
http://grammar.about.com/od/rhetoricstyle/a/stylefranklin.htm

62

Your teacher might give you *sentence combining* exercises to do that have a similar effect in helping you develop your style. The way sentence combining works is that you are presented with a series of very short sentences, called *kernels*. These kernels come in clusters of three to five sentences that are actually parts of a single sentence broken down. You will then combine these short sentences into one sentence, making decisions along the way about sentence structure and forms of words (for example, participles versus infinitives and so on). As you combine the short kernel sentences into one sentence, you get to practice making decisions that affect style, and see how you like the different options available to you as a writer. This makes you more flexible and aware of your options, so you make more informed decisions about how to phrase things and structure your sentences.

63

I like meeting with my students in conferences to look over drafts of their papers or just talk about ideas for papers. Sometimes the topics are chosen by them, and sometimes they are assigned. When I brainstorm ideas or look over drafts of papers on topics they choose, I usually start by focusing our thinking on the purpose and audience, generating fruitful conversation from questions like the following:

- What motivates you to write about this topic? Why is it interesting to you?
- What do you want your reader to get from your discussion?
- What effect do you want to have on your reader?
- What are you assuming about your reader's attitude toward the topic (and toward you)?
- What does your reader already know about the topic?
- What is s/he likely to want to know?
- How can you best arrange and phrase your material to meet the needs and expectations of your reader and be reader friendly?

52

These questions get at what writing teachers call the *rhetorical situation*, which includes

- what you want to write about (*content or argument*),
- who you're writing for (*audience or reader*), and
- how you want to project your voice as a writer (*writer*).
- With all three elements of the rhetorical situation in mind, you also need to consult your *purpose* in terms of the effect you want to have on the reader.

64

In order to figure out how best to craft your writing, you need to have a sense of purpose beyond "I have to do this writing assignment, and I want to do the best I can in order to feel good about myself or get a good grade." Many times student writers think about what makes good writing by trying to figure out "what the teacher wants." But there is a better way to approach this: figure out what you want to accomplish with a particular piece of writing, considering your purpose and your audience. Then shape your content and voice accordingly, to achieve that purpose with that audience.

With assignments where the topic is assigned, instructors might build purpose and audience into the assignment . . . and you need to focus in on that. If the purpose is not built in, speak to your teacher about it—try to find out what they're looking for you to achieve with this piece of writing. If the audience is not specified, it's often a good bet to pitch your writer's voice toward the sharpest of your peers—write in a style and with strategies to have the effect on them you're striving to achieve in your reader. After that, consider the expectations of your teacher. In this way, you will have a better basis for making decisions as a writer and a better chance of attaining a natural and compelling voice in your writing.

If you don't have an opportunity to talk with someone about these questions, it might help for you to freewrite about them. But conversation can generate a lot of pointed ideas; just be sure to have something to write with while you're talking, so you can capture the useful ideas that emerge from the talking.

65

In general, the *writing process* that is most useful for crafting academic and workplace writing is the revision-centered recursive process described above in the first section of this guidebook. But different kinds of writing assignments call for variations of the process, each geared to achieve the particular purpose of a given rhetorical situation.

Here is a suggestion for prewriting steps for an *argument paper*:

- read/annotate any assigned passages
- discuss passages and notes with peers or teacher or other adult
- reread passages, make new notes
- freewrite: play the believing/doubting game
  - o first write all the best reasons to support the position you think you want to take
  - o then write all the best reasons to support the position doubting your own
- discuss with partners or tutors/teachers/coaches your freewrites and approaches to the issue
- write out your claim precisely
- *qualify* your claim by specifying exceptions or modifications
  - o write the claim at least two ways, see what captures it most clearly, precisely, forcefully
- brainstorm supporting points, reasons, evidence, assumptions (*warrants*)
  - o make a list but don't elaborate

- freewrite reasons in support of your position
- freewrite about purpose and audience
- craft a tentative thesis
- craft a tentative outline

Following these steps will provide you with lots of good ideas and material that you can focus in a draft and then shape through revision into an effective argument. Eventually you will learn to do all of the above (and more) in a less deliberate, structured way, but to begin, it will be helpful to follow the stages listed above.

66

Adjust your writing process to your purpose, depending on what kind of writing you have to do. So, for instance, the kind of prewriting that's useful to do will vary according to the kinds of writing as follows:

- Argument:
  - o examine claims, reasons, warrants, objections/rebuttals
  - o qualify claims, warrants
- Narrative:
  - o chart the narrative arc
  - o explore telling details
- Comparison/contrast:
  - o list features of each thing
  - o identify points of comparison and contrast

67

Here is a Draft Peer Workshop Procedure for an argument paper that generates the benefits of conversation to help push revision forward:

1. With the draft facing down, the writer states his or her claim and main reasons
   a. Discuss with small peer group

2. With the draft still down, the writer states his or her strategies
    a. Discuss (teacher might have prompts to help you look at key factors)
3. Someone other than the writer, read the draft aloud
    a. Discuss (at the conceptual and organizational level, ignoring grammar, punctuation and so on)
4. Readers record responses/suggestions in phrases on response sheets and hand to the writer with a copy of the draft that may also have notes on it
5. Then on to the next writer's paper

This procedure helps writers and readers talk about the ideas in the paper and gain fresh perspectives and new ideas, while also providing opportunity to go over the draft and record comments and suggestions. Make the session as much conversation as writing notes, and let the conversation move in new directions to help the writer refocus if that seems better. The writer should also have a pen handy to record notes on her or his copy of the draft.

68

Two ways to introduce an academic paper that are better than some of those gimmicks you're sometimes encouraged to use (anecdote, quote, definition):

- identify the ongoing conversation you're joining and state your position in it.
- briefly sketch the background and relevance of the topic, keeping in mind the intended audience and purpose of the piece of writing.

69
READING PRACTICE

Here are some exercises you can use to develop your reading skill as a foundation to improve your writing:

56

- For 3-4 months read two opinion/editorial columns from the newspaper and one letter-to-the-editor per week.
  - Outline the main points and state the thesis of each column or letter.
- Then for 3-4 months: read the same as above, and now
  - state the column's or letter's thesis and write your own essay in agreement or disagreement modeled on the logic and structure of the reading.

Reading Circles
- Then for the rest of the year: continue the same reading agenda and make a reading circle—get together with others doing the same and discuss/debate in order to write your own essays, with the circle as your audience, addressing their concerns and points of view based on your discussions.
  - Then discuss those essays with each other and revise them.

70

Here's a simple three-step exercise program you can use to benefit from reading newspaper and magazine articles:
1. Annotate, outline, and summarize the essay.
2. State the purpose of the writer. Think rhetorically when you do this: what does the writer seem to want the reader to get or understand or do? What does the writer seem to be assuming about his or her reader in terms of their knowledge base and attitude toward the topic? What kind of persona is the writer projecting?
3. Journalize in two ways: first agreeing and then disagreeing with the view of the writer (writing

teachers sometimes call this approach playing the "believing-doubting game").

58

Example
Student Revision

The example below, written by a student in a College Composition class, illustrates revision in action. The writer reviewed her rough draft with an eye toward how to improve the paper through re-focusing and then revised according to a fresh understanding of her intended meaning and the potential of the draft. Look closely at the big-picture changes this student writer made in taking the paper from rough draft to final draft. This is a good example of the potential of revision.

Research Paper:
Rough Draft to Final Draft

ROUGH DRAFT

Student Name
Professor Berger
English 101 B
15 November 2012

       Living in a particular geographic location leaves certain people without a choice but to face the changes in climate or the onsets of disasters. The Philippine Islands, located off the south east of Asia, is one of those places in the world that encounters various natural weather disasters on a frequently base. The big types of disasters that the majority of the people in the Philippines encounter are typhoons and monsoons. Both of these natural disasters occur yearly and certainly cause destruction due to excessive winds or rains. Although a wide range of natural disasters strike the Philippines inevitably, the native people learn to adapt to the negative effects and make meaningful sense to the situations from which they cannot escape.

Damage of the homes and lives of people residing in the Philippines is a problem that presents when either a typhoon or monsoon hits the Philippines. People who live where the natural disaster occurs will clearly have a more significant impact on their daily lives. Having the knowledge of survival is crucial---what to do when a weather is on the way. These weather disasters become social disasters because people are affected in many different ways. Rain levels and floods have only been increasing in the Philippines as time goes on as well. Just recently in August 2012, monsoons have caused twelve continuous days of rain. Millions of people were affected and "were forced to flee the huge Shantytowns lining the rivers and sewers overnight for the safety of schools, gymnasiums, and government buildings (Singh). Levels of people's homes are not high enough to sustain the rising water levels, so therefore the schools from most of the cities become evacuation sites for those people whose homes are flooded. When tropical Storm Ondoy hit the Philippines a couple years ago, many families had to flee as well and search for evacuation sites. One lady explained her personal experience on this and described how gradually the water rose and immediately the Barangay Captain sent someone to gather the families in her city in the Philippines in an evacuation site because the dams that were built to block the waters might start to release the water (Café). Several organizations were fortunately reaching out to those families who were scarce in food and provided them with rice and other relief goods. These times are extremely difficult and some described their experience in the evacuation center as hard because "it was overcrowded" and according to this one man's experience, he explained how ten families in one room had to share two pit toilets (Café). These disasters bring people together to aid each other and help contribute to meeting their basic needs. Because of the high water levels, fish became the main source of food for several people that were able to fish them out of the water easily. Some people were fortunate enough to have family members that live in areas that were not as devastating and therefore, evacuated to their relative's homes as the storm passes through.

The after effects of any weather disaster are always unfortunate and heartbreaking for people to deal with. People in the Philippines who homes are essentially flooded or destroyed in the event must learn to rebuild their lives. People are still rescuing other people's lives from the chronic floods of the monsoons that occurred just recently especially in the metro Manila area (Singh). Lives are not going to immediately return to normal for the majority of the victims it is a process and people cope in their own individual way. Most people must reconstruct their lives and find their home again. However, some families must deal with missing or possibly deaths of family members or friends because of the disasters. These disasters affect millions of the people in the Philippines and in the past year 1,904 deaths were recorded to the Emergency Events database of the center for Research on the Epidemiology of Disasters (Singh). Another victim of tropical storm Ondoy described his experience after the disaster occurred and the problems he was now facing related to harvesting water spinach and the electrical wire system damaged from the waters. It can take many months for these families and individuals to regain their lives. Many others exert their kindness by reaching out to others who have lost lives and are rescuing those victims; they are described as "lifesavers to the multitudes who struggled to keep their heads and hopes above water" (Café). Undoubtedly, families can be torn apart from the storm because people's lives are lost. However, it is also a means for people to become closer as they learn to lean on and support one another. This brings a whole other social constructive perspective to the issue of disasters.

There is no practical way to prevent the natural disasters from occurring, but the methods of dealing with the expected situations can certainly be improved. Communities are gathering together to resolve major issue that deal with managing the effects of the Storms or other weather disasters. They have established the community-based disaster preparedness that focuses on these events and the methods of improvement. The frequency and severity of the natural disasters that occur in the Philippines are only going to increase which results in a greater impact on the millions of people living there. Establishing the base line of these problems can have a more positive effect on the outcomes. The goals of this program are to increase "the ability communities to respond promptly and flexibly to changing climate and environmental stresses" (Allen). There will be a huge emphasis on educating the people on the hazards and the strategies to prevent those. Resources will be provided ahead of time that should motivate and empower people to be more prepared.

CBDP is only a stepping stone to the broader perspective to support climate change adaptation and sustainable development (Allen). Another important consideration to the process of improving outcomes of these natural disasters is viewing the perspective of the children. Their lives are more vulnerable in these devastating situations and their role needs to be emphasized in the process of handling the situation and adapting to the changes. Participation is crucial to their understanding, preparing, and coping with natural disasters. Research has been studying methods "to capture risk perception, risk communication and action, including a short video 'adverts' for adaptation and risk reduction projects" (Tanner). Establishing these will promote protection for the children and increase communities' knowledge on the effects of these natural disasters on all people including children.

Having a foundation for dealing with these natural disasters is vital when people face them continuously in their lives. Some people are fortunate to escape but others must adapt to the climate changes. The Philippines has its advantages and disadvantages and this is a problem people are striving to overcome to deal with more effectively. Through community programs and better education of natural disasters to children can steer people in the proper direction to promote prevention and protection. There are many relief programs where people can take advantage of and work together in supporting one another.

Works Cited

Allen, Katrina M. "Community-Based Disaster Preparedness And Climate Adaptation: Local Capacity-Building In The Philippines." *Disasters* 30.1 (2006): 81-101. *Academic Search Premier*. Web. 15 Nov. 2012.

Café, Dindo P. "The Social Construction Of Disaster: Ondoy (Ketsana) In The Context Of Sagrada Familia And Inquirer.Net." *Asian Social Science* 8.10 (2012): 45-57. *Academic Search Premier*. Web. 15 Nov. 2012.

Mauch, Christof, and Christian Pfister. *Natural Disasters, Cultural Responses: Case Studies toward a Global Environmental History*. Lanham, MD: Lexington, 2009. Print.

Singh, David. " Unplanned Urbanization Increasing Flood Impacts." *UNISDR: The United Nations Office for Disaster Risk Reduction*. UNISDR, 9 Aug. 2012. Web. 1 Nov. 2012.

Tanner, Thomas. "Shifting The Narrative: Child-Led Responses To Climate Change And Disasters In El Salvador And The Philippines." *Children & Society* 24.4 (2010): 339-351. *Academic Search Premier*. Web. 15 Nov. 2012.

FINAL DRAFT

Student Name
Professor Berger
English 101 B
29 November 2012

Cultural Response to Natural Disasters

Living in a particular geographic location leaves certain
people without a choice but to face the changes in climate or the
onsets of disasters. The Philippine Islands, located off the south east
of Asia, is one of those places in the world that encounters various
natural weather disasters on a frequent basis. The big types of
disasters that the majority of the people in the Philippines encounter
are typhoons and monsoons. Both of these natural disasters occur
yearly and certainly cause destruction due to excessive winds or
rains. Although the Filipinos are faced with these frequent challenges
in their lives, they essentially rely on one another for support and
resources in rebuilding their lives, illustrating a different perspective
on the meaning of struggle yet inspiring admiration from other people
who are more fortunate enough to experience life without these
constant battles.

Knowing well strategic methods to reduce the level of
damage from natural disasters is crucial to the Filipinos who reside in
these vulnerable areas. Not all places have the same type or level of
natural disaster and every person adapts specifically to his or her
situation. Living in the Philippines for all their lives, the people
undoubtedly become accustomed to the changes that the weather
brings. Certain parts of the islands are more prone to multiple
typhoons and other parts are more prone to the monsoon seasons, but
nonetheless, either one includes excessive winds or rain. The impact
of these natural disasters is often drastic, destroying homes and
communities that lie in its paths. A most recent event occurred only a
few months ago when "a combination of the southwest monsoon and
tropical cyclones passing in the vicinity of the northern Philippines
has resulted in massive flooding in and around the Philippine capital"
("Monsoon, Tropical Cyclones"). Although there are measures taken
accordingly by the government to prepare and readily manage the
effects, the initial instincts of survival rests in the hands of the
average citizens. Weather disasters are a natural aspect of their lives

and its occurrences have become expected. Therefore, the Filipinos' way of life constantly adjusts to environmental changes. The alterations in their lifestyle due to the effects of the weather trigger an emotional response as well. One study focused on the Sagrada Familia in Calamba City, Philippines, and their experience when tropical storm Ondoy struck their location. Heavy rainfall was brought by this storm and caused many flooded homes. During the interview, members of the Sagrada Familia recalled the damage of their homes due to the rise of the water and their last resort to evacuation sites (Café 53). It is a representation of the actions of the communities, where schools and other public buildings became evacuations in various places throughout the Philippines. When other Filipino families can no longer stay in their home because of the high safety risk, they transfer to the homes of their friends or relatives.

Furthermore, planning ahead for a natural disaster has evolved through time to discover more effective methods of improving survival. In order to enhance the safety of the Filipinos when disaster strikes, everyone must be involved and participate in preparations. Adult citizens have always been heard but now the voices of the children are taken into consideration as well. This shows that communities are putting a greater effort in preparing for a natural disaster. Various ideas—such as disaster drills, risk mapping, evacuation planning, and rescue training—that incorporate their perspective were established and "showed they have a close awareness of the risks facing their lives" (Tanner 343). The main priority for the children's activities and involvement in a disaster preparation is to increase protection and reduce vulnerability (Tanner 340). This is only one aspect of how the Filipino communities will enhance their response to the weather disasters.

Generally, natural disasters do not only cause destruction physically through houses or buildings, but it can also cause destruction within a person or a family. However, the Filipinos did not fall from destruction, rather they kept their head above water and became stronger each time. Communities were able to withstand the negative effects and reach out to the people suffering after a natural disaster occurs. It is important to understand that no one should be on their own during these difficult times and "family far outweighs government or civil society institutions as a provider of safety-net support to resist shocks and stresses" (Allen 85). Many community projects are aiming to improve adaptation, mobilization, and empowerment in the peoples' lives. These times are opportunities for the Filipinos to come together to offer support and resources that others may not be able to obtain alone. The people involved are striving "to collectively identify problems, take decisions, and act on them and to allocate resources" (Allen 34). The community of the Sagrada Familia established relief programs in several places where food, money, and other necessities were provided to families in the evacuation sites (Café 55). The effort to help others makes a tremendous difference in one's life. Initially, communities do not give up on each other and only strive to assist each other more effectively.

Receiving help from others in the Filipino communities contributes to the ability to cope and adapt after a natural disaster strikes. However, the force that drives the Filipino people to move on from the event comes from within and not necessarily from others. Facing these natural disasters is a way of life for the Filipinos and most cannot escape from their situation, lacking the means of relocation. Greg Bankoff, in his theories of the coping cultures in the Philippines, discussed three valid principles that Filipinos have developed to guide them in their ways of coping. One principle is the "passive acceptance of one's fate" because they cannot control or prevent these natural disasters from occurring; another principle is "shared identity and common association" because neighbors and all are in the same boat of hardships; the third principle is "sense of humor shared by the Filipinos" because they resort to positive uplifts with laughter or jokes to reduce depression (Bankoff 270). Ultimately, Filipinos flow with the river as weather disasters continue to impact their lives. Moving forward is the only logical sense for improvement as well as failing to allow these natural disasters from taking the best of them.

Certainly, the Philippines is not the only place where a natural disaster can occur but many people, especially those living in the Americas, only encounter terrible weather disasters once or few times in their lives. Filipinos, however, must deal with this almost all their lives because it is inevitable to prevent due to its location. Some people have it tougher than others but that just means it can be a method of learning for others. Surely, there are coping strategies that people can obtain from examining the lifestyles of the Filipinos. Life brings challenges to people throughout the world and this is just the set of cards that the Filipinos are dealt with and must play with for most of their lives. It illuminates a completely new light upon life for those who have never experienced the struggles that these people are overcoming throughout their lives. Some people take their lives for granted and do not realize that they are blessed with a more fortunate life because they do not have to constantly rebuild their lives from destruction.

In essence, tropical storms or some other destructive weather can make or break people and communities, but the Filipinos have not fallen weak. This is a life-long battle that they are continuing to overcome and their strategies for achieving it are only driving in the direction of improvement. The people do not stand alone against this but are consequently joined together by the force of nature. Working together provides a more effective outcome, not only physically but psychologically as well.

Works Cited

Allen, Katrina M. "Community-Based Disaster Preparedness And
    Climate Adaptation: Local Capacity-Building In The
    Philippines." *Disasters* 30.1 (2006): 81-101. *Academic
    Search Premier*. Web. 15 Nov. 2012.

Bankoff, Greg. "Cultures of Disaster, Cultures of Coping." Ed.
    Christof Mauch and Christian Pfister. *Natural Disasters,
    Cultural Responses: Case Studies toward a Global
    Environmental History*. Lanham, MD: Lexington, 2009.
    265-84. Print.

Café, Dindo P. "The Social Construction Of Disaster: Ondoy
    (Ketsana) In The Context Of Sagrada Familia And
    Inquirer.Net." *Asian Social Science* 8.10 (2012): 45-
    57. *Academic Search Premier*. Web. 15 Nov. 2012.

"Monsoon, Tropical Cyclones Bring Massive Flooding to
    Manila." *PRECIPITATION MEASUREMENT MISSIONS*.
    National Aeronautics and Space Administration/Goddard
    Space Flight Center, 10 Aug. 2012. Web. 01 Nov. 2012.

Tanner, Thomas. "Shifting The Narrative: Child-Led Responses To
    Climate Change And Disasters In El Salvador And The
    Philippines." *Children & Society* 24.4 (2010): 339-
    351. *Academic Search Premier*. Web. 15 Nov. 2012.

Definitions

argument: an organized discussion supporting a claim with
   logical reasons, evidence and persuasive strategies

context: the background of a discussion. NOTE: This word
   does not mean *content* or *text*. Context is the
   situation in which the content appears; context is the
   issues, ideas and concerns that surround a text.

draft/drafting: A draft is a version of a paper or essay or any
   kind of writing or artistic production. Usually in the
   sense that there are multiple drafts, starting with a
   rough draft and proceeding through one or more
   revisions making subsequent drafts. The revised
   version that is turned in is known as the final draft of
   a paper. Drafting is the act of producing a draft.

essay: a short non-fiction prose discussion explaining or
   exploring ideas. NOTE: The two terms *essay* and
   story refer to different kinds of writing. An essay is
   non-fiction while a *story* is a short fiction prose work
   telling a narrative with characters and plot.

expository: informational; a kind of writing meant to explain
   or analyze a subject

narrative: a chronological discussion of a sequence of events,
   usually in prose.

prose: writing that is not poetry.

qualify/qualifier: To qualify is to change the meaning of a
   claim by making it narrower or softer. A qualifier is
   a statement that does this, often in relation to an
   essay's thesis.

revision: the act of changing the focus, central idea,
   organization or flow of a piece of writing in a large-
   scale way above and beyond the level of words and
   phrases. Revision is not concerned with correct

grammar and punctuation but with the meaning and organization of a piece of writing.

rhetoric/rhetorical: Rhetoric is the art of effective communication. Rhetorical matters are issues relating to the effectiveness of a written or verbal communication. Rhetorical strategies are ways of using language and organizing expression in order to achieve the communicator's goals in relation to his or her audience.

rote: the quality of being too mechanical in thought or expression, without bringing original and lively thought to a matter.

story: a usually short prose work telling a narrative that includes characters and plot development. Usually fiction, but we also tell non-fiction stories about our lives. NOTE: In the reading you do in school and college, a *story* is not an essay, and an *essay* is usually not a story.

thesis/thesis statement: the statement of the central idea of a piece of writing, usually stated in the introductory paragraph, and often a claim that needs to be supported in the essay that it introduces. A good thesis statement does not simply point to the topic under discussion but expresses the writer's position or main idea about the topic.

Notes

Pages 10-12 A professor of composition did a study . . .
Statistics and information from Nancy Sommers,
*Revision Strategies of Student Writers and
Experienced Adult Writers.* 12 June 1982. *ERIC.*
Web.

**Pages 13-14 two groups of writers talk about what they're
doing when they examine and revise their drafts ...**
Quotations from Nancy Sommers, "Revision
Strategies of Student Writers and Experienced Adult
Writers." *College Composition and Communication*
31.4 (1980): 378-88. Print.

Page 21 draft fearlessy, revise vigorously . . . For this pithy
formula, I am indebted to Dona J. Young, *Which
Comes First, the Comma or the Pause? A Practical
Guide to Writing,* Writer's Toolkit Publishing, 2009.
Print.

Page 31 "They Say/I Say". . . from Gerald Graff, Cathy
Birkenstein and Russell Durst, *"They Say/I Say": The
Moves That Matter in Academic Writing, with
Readings,* 2nd ed., W. W. Norton, 2011. Print.

Recommended Reading

All these resources are helpful and worthwhile, though each will not be everyone's cup of tea. Take a look and see whether you think any can be useful for you. The first one listed should belong to all people who strive to write well in college. The second belongs on the shelf of anyone who writes anything for work, including people whose work requires only emails and memos. The third is probably mostly for people who have become passionate about writing.

Michael Harvey, *The Nuts and Bolts of College Writing*. Hackett, 2003.

William Strunk Jr. and E. B. White, *The Elements of Style*. 4th edition. Longman, 2000.

Robert D. Richardson, *First We Read, Then We Write: Emerson on the Creative Process*. University of Iowa, 2009.

Those Who Helped Me Revise
(Also Known as Acknowledgments)

For their generous comments and suggestions on previous drafts, which helped me revise and improve this book, I am grateful to Alexander Berger, Andrea Berger, Barbara Berger, David Berger, Helen Berger, Cindy Carlton-Ford, Sarah Davidoff, Lisa Ede, Wayne Hall, Ron Hoag, Meghan Hollowell and Maryellen Lemieux. Thanks to Susan Berger for the great cover art and to Brianne Keith, Rob Velella and Dana Tindall for technical help with the cover. My thanks also to Catherine Delacruz for permission to print the rough and final drafts of her research paper. Good work, Catherine!

About the Author

Michael Berger has taught writing in college and high school for twenty years. In 2014 he received a Diana Hacker Award for Outstanding Programs in English from the Two-Year College English Association (TYCA) of the National Council of Teachers of English (NCTE) for developing a writing across the curriculum program in a two-year nursing college. His work with high school students has been recognized with a Leaders in Literacy Award from Cincinnati Public Schools and an Outstanding Teacher Award for high school teachers from the University of Chicago. He has taught literature and humanities surveys as well as composition and is currently Associate Professor of English and Communications at The Christ College of Nursing and Health Sciences in Cincinnati, Ohio. He has worked in corporate compliance and in marketing communications and has edited corporate, college and literary-society newsletters. He is the author of several published articles and of the book *Thoreau's Late Career and "The Dispersion of Seeds": The Saunterer's Synoptic Vision.* He holds a Ph.D. in English from the University of Cincinnati, an M.A. in English from Indiana University, and a B.A. in Liberal Arts from St. John's College.